EVERYTHING YOU DIDN'T LEARN IN SCHOOL

EVERYTHING YOU DIDN'T LEARN IN SCHOOL

———◆———

THE OFFICIAL SURVIVAL GUIDE FOR YOUNG ADULTS

Rishi Sholanki

ISBN-13: **9780995815100**
ISBN-10: **0995815100**

CONTENTS

EVERYTHING YOU DIDN'T LEARN IN SCHOOL: THE OFFICIAL SURVIVAL GUIDE FOR YOUNG ADULTS

So you've just graduated and earned your degree, and you are taking your first steps into the world of self-sufficiency—or in other words, adulthood. Congratulations from an adult who wishes to give you all the information he wishes he'd had (you're welcome). This little book aims to give you some help in making sense of adulthood, including some very important things you need to know and the institutions behind them.

For as long as you can remember, you have been in school and have successfully learned the formal and informal rules and procedures that make up the school environment. Because most of your daily life has been concentrated on school, these rules and procedures likely influence your choices, the way you regulate your time, your social interactions, the way you see yourself and others, and your vision of the future. Your years at school were important; they've set you up with some of the knowledge, skills, and perspectives you're going to need as you step into the adult world, with all of its exciting possibilities and unfamiliar responsibilities.

This world is similar; there are new rules and procedures that come into play, especially once you are earning a salary and making your own way in the world! It's up to you now to learn how to "adult" and build a foundation that will lead to many years of happiness and success. That is what we live for, right?

Each chapter in this book will cover things you will encounter as an adult. They are all very important, and having the knowledge ahead of time will do wonders toward helping you make the best decisions possible. Let's take a look at the important topics we will cover.

Chapter 1: Effective Communication in Interviews and Meetings

As a working adult, your life will include interviews and meetings. Learning how to communicate effectively in both scenarios will lead to success in your career and personal life.

Chapter 2: Learn *how* to read your pay stub and the many deductions listed on it.

You are not alone; there are many people who don't understand the different acronyms on a pay stub—now you won't be one of them.

Chapter 3: Filing a tax return? How does the CRA (Canada Revenue Agency) work?

We all file taxes, getting an understanding of how to file and the credits you can claim will save you money.

Chapter 4: Understanding common CRA documents.

The CRA does send you documents periodically. Know what they mean.

Chapter 5: Employment Rights.

You have rights as an employee! I'll explain what they are, what they mean to you, and how to ensure your future employers don't take advantage of you.

Chapter 6: Leaving Employment

So you left your job. This can be for many reasons: termination, disability, pregnancy, etc. It's best to be prepared. I'll let you know what your options are, so you can deal with challenges like this.

Chapter 7: Maternity and Parental Leave

No, maternity and parental leave are not the same thing! You might want to read this before you have kids!

Chapter 8: Buying a Car

We dive into payments and insurance.

Chapter 9: Your Rights as a Tenant

Many people rent before they own. Know your rights so you aren't taken advantage of.

Chapter 10: Buying a Home

Home ownership is a big responsibility and can be quite nerve racking. This should help calm the nerves and assist in buying a home.

Chapter 11: Mortgages

Getting a mortgage can be confusing for most. Let me break that confusion and give you a basic understanding of how mortgages work.

Chapter 12: Understanding Investment Accounts and Options

You work hard for your money. Invest it right!

Read all the chapters, or read the ones that relate to you. Either way, these are all things that you will encounter as an adult, and having the knowledge to face these things head on will keep your life moving smoothly and put you in the best possible position to succeed!

Let's head over to chapter 1, where we will start by looking at effective communication techniques.

CHAPTER 1

EFFECTIVE COMMUNICATION IN INTERVIEWS AND MEETINGS

As YOU PROBABLY already know, obtaining a job involves an interview, and maintaining a job requires many meetings. Both can be scary, but don't sweat it. You've got this! You know you are a quality employee (prospective employee). It's up to you now to communicate that in the meeting (interview). Communication is not just verbal but also visual. Here are some tips to allow you to shine like the star you are.

PREPARATION IS KEY

You may be nervous, and that's perfectly OK! This is normal. Your confidence will build the more you prepare. Even if you are not nervous, preparing is still the most important thing you can do.

FOR AN INTERVIEW
You should know what the job entails, and you should know as much as you can about the employer:

- The service or product they provide
- Their mission statement
- Where you would fit in if you got the job
- How many people they employ
- Their management or labour structure

It would be a good idea to read up on some recent news regarding the company—anything you can find.

If you are asked what you know about the company or what you like about the job, you will then have something to say. Answering with "I don't know" would put you in a lesser position, so do your best to prepare ahead of time.

For a Meeting

If you know what the meeting is about, prepare for it so you are not caught off guard with any questions that may come up. If you are not sure, speak to other colleagues who can help you prepare for the meeting by giving you information that may be required for you to complete your work.

How to Prepare for a Meeting

- Practice your presentation over and over, even with a friend, until you can present confidently.
- Prepare a list of questions that colleagues or your boss may ask.
- Have relevant facts and information (including statistics, formulas, or assumptions) ready, should you be asked to provide them.

Tips for Having a Successful Meeting

- Don't be afraid to ask questions in a meeting.
- Speak confidently.
- Jot down important notes.
- Have a list of questions prepared to ensure you get the most out of the meeting.
- Before the end of the meeting, always ask yourself, "Do I understand the expected outcome of the meeting, and does everyone understand what I presented?" If the answer is no, try to rectify that.

Meetings, whether with a few colleagues or many, are opportunities for you to show your value and leadership qualities. Be sure to make your presence known and show what you bring to the table.

FOR AN INTERVIEW

Know yourself and what's on your resume. The same applies if you're asked questions about yourself and about what you've done. Get this covered by making a list of your personal strengths and weaknesses so you can answer questions about who you are and why you are a good candidate for the job.

Make sure you know the dates and details of your previous employment. Did you receive any awards? You should have this kind of information clear in your mind so that you can answer related questions without having to think about it.

Practice interview responses. Think of some of the questions you might be asked in an interview—there are usually a few obvious ones:

- What is your greatest strength (or weakness)?
- How do you handle failure (or success)?
- How do you handle stress and pressure?
- Why do you see yourself doing well in this industry?

Think of others that may be more directly related to the job, such as:

- What do you know about this industry?
- Why are you interested in this role?

Get together with a friend or family member, and pretend you're being interviewed. This is especially important because it will help you think about possible questions and topics so that you can structure some good answers ahead of time. It will also calm your nerves and minimize the possibility of being hesitant or fumbling for words during the actual interview.

COMMON TIPS FOR MEETINGS AND INTERVIEWS

DRESS WELL
The impression you give has a lot to do with how you are dressed. If you want to be taken seriously, dress appropriately for the job and the workplace. People will take you more seriously, as it shows you take yourself and the job seriously.

LISTEN
Stay focused. You may find your attention turning to other things, such as something in the room or that lousy answer you gave to the previous question. Be aware of yourself! Be conscious of making eye contact and keeping your attention on the interviewer or person speaking so they know you are paying attention.

SPEAK CLEARLY
If you followed all of the above steps, you should be well prepared for your meeting/interview. But none of that matters if you don't speak clearly, confidently, and intelligently. How you speak is important. Do not speak too loud. Do not speak too softly. Do not mumble, say "um," or speak quickly. Basically, show that you're comfortable, confident, and up for any challenge that may be headed your way.

Of course, use formal language—no slang, street talk, or acronyms. The interviewers or people you are speaking to may not know the words or phrases, but most importantly, it suggests laziness and lack of professionalism.

Not everyone can rattle off in an eloquent sentence. In fact, most of us need time to think and process questions. That's perfectly fine. Don't be nervous or insecure because you can't answer a question within five seconds. Rather, let them know that you need to think about that one, or ask them to give you a moment, as you have so many answers to that question. In fact, taking a few moments to consider your response may even give the good impression that you are a person who does not jump in before you have thought things through.

WHAT YOU SAY WITHOUT SPEAKING

In addition to how you look and what you say, how you conduct yourself and your nonverbal communication are important as well. You might have heard of body language—our gestures and mannerisms. Here's some advice.

When entering a meeting/interview, shake hands firmly, smile, and make eye contact when you greet the interviewer/colleague/client/boss. As you sit, try not to slouch or be stiff. Just sit up normally, and lean forward a little, attentively. As the meeting goes on, avoid the urge to lean back in your chair. Depending on the distance between the chair and table, you may end up appearing too casual. Always be polite: "Yes, please," "No, thank you," etc. Listen until the speaker has finished his or her comment or question before you reply, so as not to interrupt them. Be sure to maintain eye contact. A few seconds of eye contact at a time lets the interviewer know you are listening attentively. Most importantly, smile, be positive, and show off your upbeat personality.

When leaving the meeting or interview, leave with a smile, positive attitude, and firm handshake (if called for). For those leaving an interview, don't forget to say good-bye to others in the office on your way out.

LEAVE A LASTING IMPRESSION

By communicating effectively both verbally and nonverbally, you are setting yourself up to leave a lasting impression. Such an impression is key to landing a job and eventually climbing the corporate ladder.

CHAPTER 2

HOW TO READ A PAY STATEMENT

A PAY STATEMENT (also called a pay stub, pay advice, or earning statement) is a written communication you, as an employee, receive weekly, biweekly, or monthly (depending on the pay period). Regardless of the pay period, the information on the pay stub is the same. It informs you of your pay amount, including your full pay, along with any taxes and deductions that have been made. Receiving this is a confirmation that you have been paid by your employer.

As important as this information is, it can be quite a challenge for young and old to understand the acronyms and terminology used on the statement. It may also be a bit confusing why some of the deductions are made in the first place.

In this chapter, all these questions will become answers! Amazing, right?

Fig. 1 is an example of a pay statement:

Sample company Name, 123 My Home Street, WINIPEG MB CANADA, R2W 2Y8					EARNINGS STATEMENT	
John Smith						
EMPLOYEE ID			**PERIOD ENDING**	**PAY DATE**		**CHECK NUMBER**
123456			2013/11/25	2013/11/20		321854
INCOME	**RATE**	**HOURS**	**CURRENT TOTAL**	**DEDUCTIONS**	**CURRENT TOTAL**	**YEAR TO DATE**
REGULAR	20	80	1,600.00	CPP	65.03	1,495.69
OVERTIME	25	5	125.00	EI	28.62	658.26
				INCOME TAX	305.90	7,035.70
				UNION DUES	10.84	249.32
				LIFE INSURANCE	4.94	113.62
				LONG TERM DISABILITY	7.01	161.23
				CANADA SAVING BONDS	8.00	184.00
YTD GROSS	**YTD DEDUCTIONS**		**YTD NET PAY**	**CURRENT TOTAL**	**DEDUCTIONS**	**NET PAY**
39,675.00	9,897.82		29,777.18	1,725.00	430.34	1,294.66

Common Terms and Acronyms Found on Canadian Pay Statements

Employee ID/Number: A code used by the employer to identify you and record your details.

Period Ending: The last date of the employment period for which you are being paid.

Pay Date: The date the payment was processed.

Cheque Number: If you are paid by cheque rather than by a transmission to your account, the cheque number will be stated on the pay stub. The pay stub will be attached to the cheque.

Income: What you are paid. This is expressed as either:

Gross pay: The amount you are earned before deductions. Apart from your *regular* earnings, there may also be additional *overtime* earnings. This refers to remuneration for hours worked in excess of your normal hours per week.

Net pay: What you receive after all deductions have been made—your take-home pay, in other words.

Rate: If you are paid hourly, this denotes the amount you will be paid per hour for both *regular* and *overtime* work. Note that the rate can be different for each.

Hours: If you are paid hourly, this states the number of hours you worked in the period for which you are being paid.

Current Total: This refers to the amounts that are allotted to this pay statement.

YTD: Stands for Year to Date. YTD is the total of your earnings and deductions from the beginning of the current year until today. If you add up a category's current total from each pay period, it will equal the YTD total for that category.

Deductions: The amounts withheld from your gross pay. Some of these will be *statutory deductions*—in other words, what you must pay, by law. Although compulsory, and sometimes painful, these deductions ultimately are there as much for your own benefit as they are for all of Canada's citizens.

The most common statutory deductions are as follows:

CPP: Stands for **Canada Pension Plan**. All Canadians eighteen and older contribute a percentage of their earnings to this government-administered social benefit plan. It may not seem important when you are starting out, but one day you will retire, and your CPP payments will ensure that you continue to enjoy an income and a comfortable lifestyle.

EI: Stands for **Employment Insurance**. Both you and your employer pay a small amount into this program so that if you lose your job involuntarily (layoffs, illness, or injury, failure of your employer's business, termination, or other unforeseen circumstances) you may receive EI benefits. The amount of these benefits depends on what your last salary was, how long you worked, and to some extent

Income Tax: | the employment setup in your region. Seasonal workers, for instance, such as foresters and fishermen of the Atlantic coastal region, have no work for parts of the year, and special EI rules are made for them.

This is a percentage of your pay that you (and everyone who resides in Canada), must remit to the **CRA** (Canada Revenue Agency—see chapter 4). With the tax revenue that is received from the many residents of Canada, the government funds institutions, infrastructure, benefit programs, and national and international matters that affect Canada and its citizens.

Other deductions on your pay may relate to financial security for you and your family. In fig. 1, for instance, you see that John Smith has direct deductions for *life and long-term disability insurances* and for *monthly investments* into Canadian Bonds.

Union dues are another common deduction. If you are paying union dues, be sure to speak to your union rep and find out everything your union does for you. They are there to protect your best interests, so it's a good idea to learn in what instances you can rely on them for help.

You should check your pay statement every pay period to ensure both payments and deductions are accurate. If you notice they are not, be sure to bring it up with your payroll department or manager.

Now that you understand your pay, let's dive a bit deeper into taxes and why you need to file an income tax return.

CHAPTER 3

FILING YOUR TAXES

FILING YOUR TAXES is something all residents and some nonresidents must do. Most income you receive is taxable, which means you have to pay a percentage of it to the CRA. I know we all hate paying taxes, but as mentioned before, they help fund a multitude of government institutions and benefit programs that directly or indirectly improve the lives of many Canadians.

When you begin your career, your income will probably be a salary from a Canadian employer. If, however, you start your own business, it will be the profits you make. If you are able to invest some of your money, the interest you earn from your investment may also be taxable.

Nobody likes to pay taxes, so understanding what deductions and credits you can claim will go a long way in helping you minimize the taxes you pay. But first let's look at how to file.

FILING YOUR TAXES

Each year the CRA wants to know how much taxable income you have received. You have to let them know this by filing your taxes. This is how you declare what you have earned and claim any deductions that could reduce your taxable income.

THE T1 TAX RETURN FORM

The file you make this declaration on is called a T1 form. It is described as a General Income Tax and Benefit Return form. On it, you report all your income, whether it comes from employment, self-employment (sole proprietorship or partnership), and interest on investments. Of course, you also indicate any deductions and credits you are claiming.

TAX DEDUCTIONS

When filing your taxes, there are certain expenses that you may have incurred throughout the year, which the CRA will allow you to deduct against your income, thus reducing the taxes you owe. A few common deductions you can claim are as follows:

- Qualified medical expenses
- Interest expense on loans used to invest and generate income
- Contributions to qualifying charitable organizations
- Contribution to a Registered Retirement Savings Plan (RRSP)
- Relevant use of a car (for those who are eligible)

TAX CREDITS

These are the amounts that may be deducted directly from the tax you owe. Each province may have a different set of credits, but the basic ones are as follows:

- Basic personal exemption
- Spouse or common-law partner
- Eligible dependent
- Infirm dependent
- Family caregiver
- Public Transit Passes
- Tuition

Be sure to speak to your tax preparer to ensure that you are maximizing your eligible credits.

REFUND OR BALANCE OWING

Once you enter all your information, you end up either with a refund, balance owing, or nil. If you paid too much tax, you receive a refund. If you paid not enough, you will owe. Refunds are sent by cheque or if you have direct deposit set up with CRA, it goes straight into your account.

If you owe money, you must pay them via cheque, at your bank, or through online banking.

If you owe money, you must file and pay by the deadline (usually April 30). The exception is if you are self-employed. Self-employed taxpayers must still pay their tax owing by the deadline (usually April 30) but can file their taxes later, usually by June 15.

FILING YOUR T1 FORM

There are three ways to file your T1. First, you can file through the CRA's free online system, called NETFILE, which syncs up with many of the do-it-yourself tax-preparation programs. You can also file via EFILE, whereby a qualified tax preparer will submit the tax return to CRA on your behalf. You also have the ability to paper file your tax return; however, CRA has been pushing toward online tax filing.

If you use either EFILE or NETFILE, you do not submit your supporting documents, forms, and slips with your return. You simply keep them aside in case you are asked to produce them. It's a good idea to keep any supporting documents and tax files for six years. If the CRA wants to see these documents at some point within the six years, they will send you a letter asking for them.

If you choose to mail your T1, you can download it from CRA's free software tax preparation program. Your slips, receipts, and other documents that support your claims do not need to be included, but, as with electronic filing, keep them safe in case the CRA asks for them.

DIY OR GET PROFESSIONAL HELP

You can self-file by paper or through one of the tax preparation software programs available to you. If your income and deductions are relatively simple, there should be no problem. But if you are unsure of anything, especially what deductions and credits you might be able to claim, it is always wise to get a professional tax expert to file for you. Yes, it costs money; however, it saves you time and energy from having to figure out for yourself what to claim and how to claim it. They may also be able to uncover credits/deductions you may not be taking advantage of.

At the end of the day, your goal is to maximize credits and deductions to ultimately pay the least amount of tax—or maybe no tax at all!

HELPFUL LINKS

For more information on income tax and taxation in general, check out the Canada Revenue Agency website: http://www.cra-arc.gc.ca/

CHAPTER 4

UNDERSTANDING COMMON CRA DOCUMENTS

ONCE YOU FILE your tax return, you will receive a number of important documents from the CRA. It is important you understand what they are. In this brief chapter, I will introduce them to you.

NOTICE OF ASSESSMENT

After you have filed your tax return (T1), the CRA will acknowledge they have received and processed your return by issuing you a Notice of Assessment. This document provides you a summary of income earned, credits applied, taxes paid, and the end result of your filing—refund or balance owing. It will also indicate if any adjustments to your filing were made, provide you information on any carry-forward credits that you may claim in the future, and provide you a summary of your RRSP contribution limit. For those who have participated in the Home Buyers' Plan or Lifelong Learning Plan (see chapter 12), you will also see your balances for these programs.

NOTICE OF REASSESSMENT

This is a notice you will receive if the CRA has adjusted your return, whether it was done via the Beneficial Client Adjustment Initiative, because you requested it via T1 Adjustment, or because information when filing was incorrect and an adjustment needed to be made.

T1 REVIEW LETTER

Sometimes the CRA selects taxpayers to be audited. If you happen to be one of them, they will send you a letter requesting any documents they need from you to support your claims. They will then do their audit. If they find no reason to change the original assessment, there will be no further action. However, if your return has changed as a result of the audit, the CRA will send you a Notice of Reassessment. This will tell you what additional taxes you must pay, as well as any penalties that might be applicable. There could also be the case where a reassessment results in a refund to you, with taxable interest.

BENEFICIAL CLIENT ADJUSTMENT INITIATIVE

This program allows the CRA to match the information you submitted with the information provided by other involved parties, such as your employer or financial institution. They do this to discover if there are discrepancies that need to be investigated or if there was an error in filing which could have resulted in a positive difference for you.

The Matching Program also compares information on the returns filed by your spouse or common-law partner and eligible dependents to determine your GST/HST credits, Guaranteed Income Supplement, and other family-related benefits provided by the government.

T1 ADJUSTMENT

If you find that you made a mistake when filing your return, missed relevant credits or deductions, or forgot to include a slip, you can file a T1 adjustment, asking the CRA to adjust your filed tax return. The CRA will review the submitted information and may request more information. Then they will give their decision of whether they will accept the adjustment fully, partially, or not at all. They will usually provide you with a Notice of Reassessment and an explanation of what changes were made. If your T1 Adjustment was not accepted, they will send you a letter indicating why.

THE GST/HST CREDIT

The Goods and Services Tax (GST) and Harmonized Sales Tax (HST) are both value-added taxes. Depending on where you live in Canada, you automatically pay one of these taxes each time you buy something.

To assist persons or families with low or modest incomes, the government pays them a quarterly tax-free amount that offsets some or all of the GST or HST that they pay. You don't have to apply for this credit. The CRA automatically sees if you are eligible for it when you file your tax return (T1).

These are just some of the common documents you will encounter from the CRA. If you do receive a document that you are unfamiliar with, be sure to speak to a tax specialist about it.

HELPFUL LINKS

For more information on relevant CRA documents or the GST/HST credit, check out the Canada Revenue Agency website: http://www.cra-arc.gc.ca/

CHAPTER 5

EMPLOYMENT RIGHTS

As a young adult, finding work may be difficult. We often take jobs that fall outside of a standard nine-to-five salary-paying job with a large employer. Many young adults work for small businesses and start-ups, where perhaps they are getting paid an hourly wage instead of a salary. With the many different types of employment and work environments young adults find themselves in, it is imperative to know your rights as an employee.

EMPLOYMENT STANDARDS

If you work for a federally regulated business, then your labour rights are covered under the Canada Labour Code. If you do not work for a federally regulated business, then you must follow the standards set by your province or territorial ministry of labour. Some of the more common employment standards cover your rights regarding:

PAY
In each province or territory, there is a fixed *minimum wage*. Employers may pay an employee more than this, but never less.

Employees must be paid by specified dates or at regular intervals and receive a *pay statement* showing their wages and deductions for that pay period.

HOURS OF WORK AND OVERTIME PAY
A standard workweek in Canada is between thirty-five and forty hours. However, overtime pay starts when an employee works in excess of the

prescribed set out of hours set by their employer, and the regulation they fall under. The extra pay for overtime work is usually around 1.5 times the normal pay rate. Employers cannot refuse to pay the rate legislated by the provincial or territorial authorities.

Vacation Time and Vacation Pay
Generally, employees are entitled to an annual vacation with full pay. How much time you get depends on where in Canada you live and your employer's benefit package. In British Columbia, Alberta, Manitoba, Ontario, and Québec, for example, workers get a minimum of two weeks off.

Public Holidays
Some public holidays depend on where in Canada you live and work, and others are national and even international, like Christmas or New Year's Day. On these days, employees are entitled to a day off. Those who do work on these days may claim overtime pay.

Coffee and Meal Breaks
There are rules about how many breaks employees may take during a working day and how long these breaks must be. It is fairly standard for employers to allow a half-hour break for every five hours of consecutive work.

Pregnancy and Parental Leave
In chapter 2, I told you that the acronym EI on your pay stub stands for Employment Insurance and that paying it entitles you to benefits if you become unemployed.

It also offers benefits to mothers who are off work because they recently gave birth and to new parents caring for a newborn or a recently adopted child (we will discuss this at length in chapter 7).

Personal Emergency Leave and Family Medical Leave
You have a right to take Personal Emergency Leave and Family Medical Leave. This will be discussed further in chapter 6.

TERMINATION NOTICE AND TERMINATION PAY

Termination simply means that the relationship between employer and employee has come to an end. If the employer ends the relationship, then the employee becomes entitled to a period of notice or payment in lieu of notice.

This does not apply, however, if the employer can prove *just cause* for dismissing the employee. Just cause includes criminal acts, gross incompetence, willful misconduct or defiance, and breach of workplace policy on the part of the employee.

The obligation to give notice or payment in lieu of notice also does not apply if the worker voluntarily resigns from the job.

As indicated in the chart below (fig. 2) the amount of notice or payment in lieu of notice required depends on the length of time the employee has worked for the employer.

LENGTH OF EMPLOYMENT	LENGTH OF NOTICE
3 months but less than 1 year	one week
1 year or more but less than 3 years	two weeks
3 years or more but less than 4 years	three weeks
4 years or more but less than 5 years	four weeks
5 years or more but less than 6 years	five weeks
6 years or more but less than 7 years	six weeks

EXCEPTIONS

Not all workers have the same rights; some may be subject to variations. For piece-rate workers, for instance (such as farm workers), there is no minimum wage and no public holiday pay. Fishers, loggers, oil workers, home-care providers, doctors, lawyers, and accountants are all subject to different employment rights.

HEALTH AND SAFETY IN THE WORKPLACE

All provinces and territories have laws that protect workers from workplace conditions that pose a risk to the health and safety of workers.

While each act is different, they all include the basic right of workers to refuse a task they consider dangerous to themselves and/or their coworkers. Once workers report such a refusal, the employer is obliged to investigate the matter. All provinces and territories have legislated *worker's compensation* benefits. If, due to his or her job, a worker is injured or becomes sick, he or she is entitled to these benefits. Any accident or event must be reported to the employer or supervisor, and a medical professional must be called. A claim is then filed with the *worker's compensation board.*

THE HUMAN-RIGHTS FACTOR

The law makes provisions for the general protection of basic human rights, including in the workplace. When hiring workers, employers may not take advantage or refuse candidates on the basis of race, cultural background, religious affinity, sexual orientation, gender, age, disability, or marital status. If they do, it is called discrimination. Discrimination is illegal.

Harassment, which is a form of discrimination, is also illegal. Harassment usually persists over time and involves unwanted physical or verbal behaviour that offends you or humiliates you.

If you experience anything that feels like discrimination or harassment, take the matter first to your employer, who should respond and make every effort to resolve the matter. If it cannot be resolved at that level, you should then go to your union, if you are a member of one. If not, then you should speak to the provincial or territorial human rights commission or the Canadian Human Rights Commission. Your Provincial Ministry of Labour also has a lot of helpful information to assist you in addressing these issues.

HELPFUL LINKS

For more information on the following resources, please check their websites
Canadian Human Rights Commission:

http://www.chrc-ccdp.ca/

Canada Labour Code and How to Find Out If You Are a Federally Regulated Employee

http://www.esdc.gc.ca/en/jobs/workplace/human_rights/employ-ment_equity/regulated_industries.page

Federal Labour Standards:

http://www.esdc.gc.ca/en/jobs/workplace/employment_standards/labour/index.page

Health and Safety:

http://www.labour.gc.ca/eng/health_safety/index.shtml

Link to Your Provincial and Territorial Labour Standards:

http://www.cic.gc.ca/english/work/labour-standards.asp

Other Labour-Related Inquiries:

http://www.labour.gc.ca/eng/home.shtml

CHAPTER 6

LEAVING EMPLOYMENT–PERMANENT OR TEMPORARILY

AT SOME POINT in time, you may have to leave your employment due to termination or various personal circumstances. Knowing your rights when you leave employment will give you the confidence you need to handle the stressful situation of being off work. Here are the most common scenarios that you will come across when it comes to leaving employment.

INVOLUNTARY LOSS OF WORK

If you lose your job, you may be entitled to Employment Insurance (EI) benefits. These are known as regular benefits, and you are eligible to receive them if you

- lost your job through no fault of your own;
- were employed in insurable employment;
- have worked the required number of insurable hours over the past fifty-two weeks;
- are available and willing to work daily and can show, by keeping written records, that you are actively seeking work; or
- have been without work or pay for a minimum of seven consecutive days during the past fifty-two weeks.

It is important to apply for your benefits as soon as you become unemployed. After four weeks, if you have not claimed your benefits, you may lose them.

Step-by-step instructions on how to apply for EI, and the forms you must submit are available on the Service Canada website. You can apply online or at one of the Service Canada locations.

Did you know?
Teachers can apply for EI during the summer months in between school years.

VOLUNTARY LOSS OF WORK

You will not be entitled to benefits if you left your job by your own choice unless you can prove just cause. Just cause usually involves the following two scenarios.

SCENARIO 1
A situation at work has become so intolerable, and interventions are nonexistent or so ineffective that you had no other reasonable choice but to leave. Such situations include the following:

- Sexual or other harassment
- Discrimination
- Hazardous or unhealthy working conditions
- Major changes in the terms and conditions of your job that affect wages or salary
- Excessive overtime or an employer's refusal to pay for overtime work
- Major changes in work duties
- Difficult relations with a supervisor, for which you are not primarily responsible
- Your employer is doing things which break the law
- Discrimination because of membership in an association, organization, or union of workers
- Pressure from your employer or colleagues to quit your job

<u>SCENARIO 2</u>

A change in your family or personal circumstances makes it no longer possible to continue in your job. This may include the following:

- Needing to move with a spouse or dependent child to another place of residence
- Having to provide care for a child or another member of your immediate family
- Reasonable assurance of another job in the immediate future

JUST CAUSE DISMISSAL

You will also not be able to claim EI benefits if you are dismissed and your employer can prove just cause for doing so. This would include if you were guilty of

- misconduct;
- gross incompetence; or
- breach of workplace policy.

PERSONAL EMERGENCY LEAVE

The type of leave you are entitled to depends upon whether you work in a federally regulated sector. If you are not in a federally regulated sector, then your province and territory have their own standards when it comes to personal emergency leave. Your entitlement for personal emergency leave can be from days to weeks. Be sure to check out the *helpful links* below to look up what type of leave applies to you.

FAMILY MEDICAL LEAVE

Family Leave allows you to take extended time away from work to provide care or support to certain family members who have an illness. Although your employer does not pay you during this period, it is job-protected, and once again, the EI has you covered. It will pay up to 100 percent of your pay for a period of six weeks.

SICK LEAVE

If you are sick, and in a federally regulated sector, you are entitled to sick leave protection up to seventeen weeks, provided that you have been working for the same employer for at least three consecutive months. Upon fifteen days of returning to work, you must provide your employer (if they request one) with a medical certificate.

MATERNITY AND PARENTAL LEAVE

This is a biggie, so I decided to make its own chapter and dive into it in more detail. Chapter 7 will be on this topic.

EI BENEFITS

In many of the above cases, you may be eligible to receive EI benefits while off work, on leave. There are two types—EI Regular Benefit and EI Sickness Benefit. Check out the *Helpful Links* for an overview and eligibility requirements.

SELF-EMPLOYED INDIVIDUALS

If you are self-employed and are not paying into EI currently, you are not eligible to receive EI benefits during the above-mentioned leave periods. However, you could register for EI Special Benefits, whereby you register with Government of Canada and pay into EI every year. By doing so, and meeting the eligibility criteria, you will receive EI Special Benefits due to the following type of leave:

- Maternity benefits
- Parental benefits
- Sickness benefits
- Compassionate care benefits
- Parents of critically ill children benefits

HELPFUL LINKS

For more information on leaving employment, check out the following sites:

For different types of employment leave for federally regulated employees:

http://www.esdc.gc.ca/en/jobs/workplace/employment_standards/labour/leave.page?

For a step-by-step guide on applying for EI, check out the Service Canada Website:

http://www.servicecanada.gc.ca/eng/video/ei.shtml

To make an application for Employment Insurance (EI) online:

http://www.esdc.gc.ca/en/ei/apply.page

EI Regular Benefit—Overview, Eligibility and FAQ

http://www.esdc.gc.ca/en/ei/regular_benefit/index.page?

EI Sickness Benefit—Overview, Eligibility and FAQ:

http://www.esdc.gc.ca/en/ei/sickness/index.page?

EI Special Benefits for Self-Employed Individuals—Overview, Eligibility and FAQ:

http://www.esdc.gc.ca/en/reports/ei/self_employed_special_benefits.page#h2.1-h3.1

Your Provincial or Territorial Ministries of Labour:

http://www.cic.gc.ca/english/work/labour-standards.asp

CHAPTER 7

MATERNITY AND PARENTAL LEAVE

No, THEY ARE not the same thing! Keep reading!

HOW IT WORKS

Straightforward *maternity leave* is an EI benefit available to *biological mothers*. The maximum EI benefit is for fifteen weeks. As of 2017, it may start up to eight weeks before the expected date of delivery and can end as late as seventeen weeks after the actual birth. Surrogate mothers and mothers who put their babies for adoption are also eligible. You will need to give proof of your pregnancy by signing a statement declaring the anticipated due date or the date of birth.

All parents of newborn or newly adopted children are entitled to *parental leave*. It can be taken any time during the baby's first year of life for a period of up to thirty-five weeks. This can be shared between the parents. *Parental leave* can be taken in conjunction with or independently of *maternity leave,* but the total leave cannot exceed fifty-two weeks.

WHO QUALIFIES?

To qualify for these EI benefits, you must meet the following criteria:

- You must have given birth to, or adopted a baby (parental leave only) or be expecting a baby.

- You must have worked at least six hundred insurable work hours during the qualifying period.
- You must have stopped working.
- You meet the specific criteria for receiving EI maternity or parental benefits.
- Your normal weekly earnings are reduced by more than 40 percent.

APPLYING

You can apply for EI maternity benefits before you give birth. In fact, you can start receiving benefits during the eighth week before your due date or before the actual week you give birth.

If you apply for benefits later than four weeks after your last day of work, you risk losing benefits.

For adoptive parents, benefits start from the date the child is placed with them. The cut-off date for applying for maternity benefits is seventeen weeks after the anticipated week of birth or the week of actual birth, whichever comes later.

If you decide to start early, it is necessary to inform Service Canada by telephone (1-800-206-7218) and tell them your baby's birth date once he or she arrives.

To apply, you must submit an application online on the Service Canada website, where you will be taken step-by-step through the application process. You will need the following information:

- Social Insurance Number (SIN)—if yours starts with a nine; you will need to show proof of your immigration status and work permit
- Mother's maiden name
- Mailing and residential addresses
- Banking information

Note: as of 2017 there is only a one-week waiting period before you will receive any EI payments.

HOW MUCH EI BENEFIT?

The basic rate of benefits payments is 55 percent of your average weekly pay up to the maximum amount. As of 2017, the maximum weekly payment is $537. Payments are taxable.

TO SUMMARIZE

To recap, you may receive EI maternity benefits up to eight weeks prior to the expected date of birth and not beyond seventeen weeks after the week you were expected to give birth or the week you gave birth, whichever is the latest. EI maternity leave will be paid for a maximum of fifteen weeks.

You may receive EI parental benefits for a maximum of thirty-five weeks, which must end fifty-two weeks after the week your child was born or was placed with you for adoption.

Either parent can take parental leave, or it can be split how the couple sees fit, but it cannot go past the maximum thirty-five weeks.

IMPORTANT INFORMATION TO KEEP IN MIND

Keep in mind that these numbers above relate to your EI benefit period and do change periodically. The number of weeks of unpaid leave you may take differs based upon the province or territory you reside in. The conditions for receiving EI may also change. Service Canada is usually the best site to find out information related to EI Maternity and Parental Leave questions. Below you will find *Helpful Links* to keep you informed.

HELPFUL LINKS

For more information on Maternity and Parental leave, check out the following websites:

EI Maternity and Parental Leave benefits (including eligibility criteria):

http://www.esdc.gc.ca/en/ei/maternity_parental/index.page?

EI Maternity and Parental Leave—FAQ:

http://www.esdc.gc.ca/en/reports/ei/maternity_parental.page

Applying for EI benefits:

http://www.esdc.gc.ca/en/ei/apply.page

Maternity and Parental Leave by Province or Territory:

http://www.cic.gc.ca/english/work/labour-standards.asp

CHAPTER 8

BUYING A CAR

So you just filed your taxes and received a big refund. Now you want to buy a car. There are two ways you can do that, and it's not always easy to decide between them. Your options are to choose between financing and leasing.

WHAT'S THE DIFFERENCE?

When you lease you are essentially only paying for the depreciation of the vehicle's value over the period of the lease (plus interest). If the list price is $30,000 and the deprecation during the three-year lease is $10,000, the total cost to you would be $10,000 plus interest spread over the three years. As you can see this is a lot cheaper than having to pay the full $30,000.

If you finance the car, you have to take out a loan for the full price of $30,000 and pay it back over the term of the loan, plus interest. If you do the math, the monthly lease payments could be less than half of the finance payments, but at the end of the term, you do not own the car.

On the other hand, if you choose to finance it, the car becomes yours after it's paid off, and your monthly payments cease altogether. If you lease, you will have to pay monthly payments as long as you want to have a car; when your first car reaches its final lease date, you can exchange it for another or buy it outright.

If you like the idea of driving a new car every three or four years, with pretty low maintenance costs, leasing may be attractive for you.

If you are happy to keep your car for more than five years and to drive debt free, then financing is best for you.

There are quite a few things to consider, so take your time to work out which option would be best for you.

CAR INSURANCE

Whatever you decide, you are required by law to have auto insurance. It's a good idea before you sign the lease or the purchase contract to investigate the insurance coverage and premiums that come with owning a car. You might even find it will influence the kind of car you end up buying, as the insurance premium on the car you wanted may be so expensive that you decide to buy something else or nothing at all!

While car insurance is compulsory, there are a number of good reasons why you would want it. First and foremost, it offers protection against liability you might incur as a result of an accident with another party. It also provides financial protection, in the form of covering the costs or repairs if the vehicle is damaged in an accident, from some other peril, or stolen.

HOW TO GET INSURED

The best way to get insured is to speak to a few brokers or agents (a broker usually represents a few companies and can provide many options, while an agent usually sells policies for one company). There are many possibilities, and premiums vary from insurer to insurer, so shop around. Don't just take the lowest rate; the lower the premium, the less coverage you get. Go for the best coverage you can get for a price you can afford.

You can also go online, and at your own convenience, check out different companies' or brokers' websites. Most brokerages offer phone quotes, so getting insured is fairly easy.

To be insured you need to provide the following:

- Canadian driving license details
- Name and address
- Make and model of the vehicle
- Details about any past and current insurance providers

The form below (fig. 3) will give you some idea of what questions to expect when speaking with an insurance broker.

Your Car	
Make:	Model:
Year:	Distance driven one way to work:
Annual kilometers driven:	Do you use your car for business? Y N
Vehicle Identification Number (VIN):	
Your Current Broker, Agent, or Insurance Company	
Name:	Company:
Phone:	Insurance policy number:
Coverage:	Deductibles:
Your current annual insurance rate:	
You (as principal driver)	
Gender:	Birth Date:
Marital Status:	
Number of years you have been licensed to drive in Canada or the U.S.:	
Your driver's license number:	
Has your policy ever been canceled for non-payment or any other reason?	
First-time driver? Y N	

Did you receive a Driver Training Certificate? Y N	
List details of all accidents and claims in the past 6 years:	
List details of all traffic violations (not including parking tickets) in the past 3 years:	
Coverages:	Deductibles:
Other (Occasional) Drivers	
Gender:	Birth Date:
Marital Status:	
Number of years licensed to drive in Canada or the U.S.:	
Did they receive driver training? Y N	Do they have a Driver Training Certificate? Y N
List details of all accidents and claims in the past 6 years.	
List details of all traffic violations (not including parking tickets) in the past 3 years.	

YOUR PINK CARD

Once you have completed the purchase of your insurance, the documents will be sent to you with a proof of insurance—a pink card that should fit into your wallet and should be kept with you whenever you are driving. You could receive a ticket if you are caught driving without insurance.

Once insured, if you have to make a claim, be completely honest with your insurance company. Any of the following is considered fraud:

- Lying about what really happened
- Filing bogus accident or damage claims
- Including older damage when submitting a claim
- Withholding information and details about previous accidents or traffic violations
- Receiving payments for treatments you never had

If you are found to be committing fraud,

- your claim will be denied;
- your policy may be canceled;
- your premiums will go up;
- you may be denied insurance in the future; or
- you can be fined heavily or spend up to two years in prison.

TYPES OF CAR-INSURANCE COVERAGE

There are three basic types of insurance coverage.

Third party liability covers, up to a certain amount, any damage you may cause to another person's property, or compensation for death or injury of another person. The minimum amount of third-party liability insurance you must be covered for is $200,000 in all provinces and territories except Quebec, where it is $50,000. However, most drivers choose $1,000,000, and many companies will offer $1,000,000 as their minimum coverage.

Collision insurance covers damage to your own car in the case of an accident that is your fault.

Comprehensive insurance covers you against theft and vandalism in addition to collision and third-party liability.

In recent years, many other optional benefits have become available—so many, in fact, that even the brokers have trouble keeping up. Be sure to ask your insurance broker about these optional coverages, as you do not want to be in a position where you thought you had coverage for a claim, when in fact you don't.

YOUR DEDUCTIBLE

Depending on your type of coverage or your degree of fault, your insurance company may not pay the whole cost of damages and may require you to pay something toward your loss. This is called your deductible.

HOW TO GET THE BEST RATES

There are a few things you, as a young driver, can do to get better insurance rates:

- Take a driving-training course from a recognized driving instructor.
- Ask your insurance company if they offer any student or alumni discounts.
- Keep your driving record clean and free of at-fault accidents and traffic violations.

I know insurance for a young adult can be expensive, but it's definitely worth having. The good news is that once you hit twenty-five years old, the rates should start declining as you move into a different driver class.

Note: Car-insurance coverage, premiums, and minimum requirements will vary based upon the province or territory you live in. Be sure to speak to a qualified insurance professional to receive the most up-to-date and accurate information regarding your insurance coverage.

HELPFUL LINKS

For more information on mandatory insurance coverage in Canada, check out the following websites:

Insurance Bureau of Canada

http://www.ibc.ca/nl/auto

CHAPTER 9

YOUR RIGHTS AS A TENANT

PART OF BECOMING independent is moving into your own home. While we would all love to buy a home, most likely you will start by renting an apartment or house. By doing so you become a tenant. The person or company you rent from is the *landlord*. Both parties have rights and responsibilities, and it is essential that you know what these are.

All the terms and rules will be covered in your *rental agreement* or *lease*. Read it carefully. Having the right information will prepare you for any issue that might arise. Legislation is similar throughout Canada, but each province or territory may vary in the way it interprets the rules. You will need to know the specific landlord and tenant laws where you live.

WHERE TO LEARN ABOUT LANDLORD-TENANT LAWS IN YOUR PROVINCE OR TERRITORY

Newfoundland & Labrador
Website:

Service NL
http://www.servicenl.gov.nl.ca/

Prince Edward Island

Website:

Office of the Director of Residential Rental Property
http://www.irac.pe.ca/rental

Nova Scotia
Website:

Access Nova Scotia
http://novascotia.ca/sns/access/

New Brunswick   The Office of the Rentalsman
Website: http://www.snb.ca/irent/

Quebec   Regie du Logement
Website: http://www.rdl.gouv.qc.ca/

Ontario   Landlord & Tenant Board
Website: http://www.sjto.gov.on.ca/ltb/

Manitoba   Residential Tenancies Branch
Website: http://www.gov.mb.ca/cca/rtb/

Saskatchewan   Office of Residential Tenancies
                         (Rentalsman)
Website: https://www.saskatchewan.ca

Alberta   Service Alberta
Website: *http://www.servicealberta.gov.ab.ca/*

British Columbia   Residential Tenancy Branch
Website: http://www2.gov.bc.ca/gov/content/
                         housing-tenancy

Yukon   Residential Tenancies Office
Website: http://www.community.gov.yk.ca/
                         consumer/rto.html

Northwest Territories   Department of Justice, NWT Rental Office
Website: http://nwthc.gov.nt.ca/

Nunavut   Department of Justice
Website: http://www.gov.nu.ca/justice

Note: The websites listed above may change; however, a quick Google search will get you to the information you are looking for.

RULES YOU SHOULD FIND OUT ABOUT

SECURITY DEPOSIT LIMITS AND DEADLINES IN YOUR PROVINCE
Your landlord may require a security deposit. This usually amounts to one month's rent or an agreed-upon value, which the landlord holds onto until you move out. It's intended to cover any damage to the premises beyond normal wear and tear and to compensate the landlord if you should leave unexpectedly without paying. Be sure to check the laws in your province or territory, as in some provinces like Ontario, a landlord cannot ask for a security deposit other than the last month's rent.

GETTING YOUR DEPOSIT BACK
Unless there are expenses for damage you have caused, the landlord is obligated to return your deposit when you leave—assuming the deposit was more than the last month's rent.

RENT DUE DATES
Which day of the month is rent due? When is it considered late?

IF YOU CAN'T PAY RENT ON TIME
There are steps you can take if you find yourself in the situation of not being able to pay your rent by the due date. Approach your landlord to negotiate a partial payment or delayed agreement. If you don't speak to your landlord, he or she can start making a motion to evict you.

WHAT IF YOU ARE RENTING A PLACE WITH OTHERS?
Perhaps you will be sharing your apartment with others. It's a good idea, after all, because it means each person pays less rent, and the workload

is divided up. If you all sign the lease or rental agreement, then you are cotenants, and there are some things you should know about being cotenants.

Cotenants are *jointly and severally liable* for all the responsibilities of tenancy. That means you are all responsible, and you are individually responsible. In other words, while each of you may agree to pay a certain part of the rent, if one of you can't pay, the landlord can demand the full rent from you or one of the others. If one of you damages something, each of you can be held responsible. You get the picture. To cover yourselves, you should go beyond just casual or verbal agreements and undertakings. You should make sure that everyone fully understands what they have signed up for. A good idea is to draw up a written agreement among the cotenants covering the following:

- Everyone's share of the rent
- Occupancy of each room
- Allocating communal rooms
- Allowances and limitations for guest stayovers—significant others, for instance?
- A cleaning schedule where everyone knows when and for what they are responsible for
- The time of night that noise should stop or be minimized
- What to do if one of you decides to move out
- Handling disagreements about household matters
- How to fairly handle the removal of an undesirable roommate

DISCRIMINATION

Discrimination based on race, religion, national origin, familial status, disability, or sex is prohibited by federal housing laws. Some provinces have specifically included other possible areas of discrimination.

REPAIRS

Generally, the landlord has to supply and maintain certain services and keep the structure of the building safe and in good condition. The landlord's responsibilities include the following:

- The integrity of floors, roofs, window and door frames, staircases, outside walls, etc.
- Electricity, heating, and plumbing systems
- Hot and cold water
- Extermination of pests

If, however, your own negligence or carelessness is the cause of the problem, you will most likely receive the bill, or it will be deducted from your security deposit.

That takes care of the big stuff—the major repairs. What about the little things that can spoil the quality of living: the dripping faucet, fading or discoloured wall paint, loose tiles, loose floorboards, or mildewed grout? These don't make the place uninhabitable; they are just not pleasant to live with.

Does your landlord have to repair these too? There is no straightforward answer. It will depend on many factors, including the nature of the problem itself, the terms of the agreement or lease, any extra verbal or written undertaking your landlord has committed to, and, of course, what the landlord-tenant laws of the province or territory say.

If you are fairly convinced that a landlord is responsible for a specific repair, you may simply phone or visit him or her and ask that the person take care of it. If there is no response, you should follow the steps indicated by your provincial or territorial tenancy board/office.

TENANTS' RIGHTS TO PRIVACY

The landlord may enter the property you rent from him or her only under certain circumstances. These are generally confined to the following:

- Assessing the property for repairs
- Making repairs
- Responding to an emergency
- Conducting an inspection
- Showing the premises to prospective tenants or buyers

The landlord is required to give advance notice if he or she does, for whatever reason, intend to visit. Usually this is twenty-four hours, and the person must enter the property during a certain time period— usually 8:00 a.m. to 8:00 p.m.

EVICTIONS AND TERMINATIONS

Eviction basically means that you are asked to leave because you have done something that violates the lease agreement. In order to evict you, your landlord must end the tenancy by giving you adequate and formal written notice.

If you do not comply with any of these notices, either by leaving or by removing the reason for your eviction (paying the rent you owe, for example), the landlord can take legal action against you and file a motion for your eviction. If he or she can prove you broke the lease agreement or did not do something you were obligated by agreement to do, the board may rule that you must leave the premises.

Termination without cause occurs when the landlord writes to ask you to move without having to give a reason, as long as you are notified a minimum sixty days prior to your lease agreement ending.

While this information is meant to keep you informed, it does vary based upon the tenancy laws where you reside. Be sure you read and understand your rights as a tenant to ensure you make the most of your tenancy and to ensure you are not taken advantage of.

CHAPTER 10

BUYING A HOME

AT SOME POINT, if not now, you will want to buy and move into your own home. Let's look at what that entails.

The first thing you'll do is look for the right home. You'll scour the Internet and your neighborhood for "for sale" signs, open houses, and new housing developments. However, if you're wise, you'll contact a Realtor. Realtors will help you look for a property and save you the time and energy of doing it yourself. Usually when you are on the buy side, Realtors' services are free, as they usually get paid by the seller of the property. Not only can Realtors help you search for properties, but they can also provide you relevant information on the properties you are viewing and information on the area and market you are looking at. In addition to this, they work for you and represent your interests.

Once you find a property you want to buy, you will put in an *offer to purchase.* Here's where a Realtor becomes really useful because they know how to prepare the offer for you.

If the seller accepts your offer, you shake hands and move on to the next step.

If the seller does not accept your offer, they may make a *counter-offer,* usually with a few new conditions or changes to the existing one. Considering what you can afford, you can either accept the counter-offer or make another counter-offer. This will continue, back and forth, until both parties agree to a mutually acceptable offer or until one party walks away from the deal.

CLOSING DAY

The day you take legal possession of your new home is called closing day. On this day, any outstanding requirements are completed. Any additional deposits, mortgage funds, and adjustments are gathered by your lawyer and wired to the seller's lawyer to complete the transaction. Congrats! You've just bought your home. Here are the keys!

HIDDEN COSTS

LAWYER'S FEE:
Your lawyer is hired to review the terms of the contract, conduct title searches, review status certificates (condos), and provide a legal opinion on the purchase of the property. He or she will then complete the purchase transactions on the closing date, including registering your name on the title, and transferring funds to the seller's lawyer. As you can see, having a real-estate lawyer is a must!

Hiring one will cost around $600 to $2,000.

LAND-TRANSFER TAX
Depending on where in Canada you live, you may be charged some variation of a land-transfer tax. This is based upon the province, territory, and municipality you live in. It could come to a considerable amount, so find out ahead of time, and make sure it is factored into your budget.

Some provinces and municipalities offer eligible first-time buyers of new and resale homes a rebate of the provincial land-transfer tax. In Ontario you can receive up to $2,000, and an additional $3,725, if you purchase a home in Toronto.

Home Inspection
This will cost around $500, but it's worth it to know if there are major deficiencies in the house before you close the deal.

Real-Estate Fees
As mentioned earlier, when you buy a home, you usually do not have to pay real-estate fees to your Realtor, as the seller is responsible for that. Be sure to confirm this if you are on the buy side of the transaction. If you are on the sell side, you may have to pay up to 5 percent in real-estate commissions. Be sure to find out the fees ahead of time and try to negotiate a lower listing commission as best as possible.

Rental Items
Purchasing property may also come with rental items that you will now assume—such as a furnace, hot water tank, air conditioner, or alarm system. Since these are usually monthly items, you must factor them into your budget. You should find out how long the term of the contract is and if there are any final lump sum payments at the end of the contract, as you will be responsible for those too.

Common Adjustments
These are also part of your closing costs. For example, if you buy a house in June and the seller has already paid the property taxes for the entire year, you will have to reimburse the seller for the months you live in the house. These common adjustments are tallied by your lawyer, who will provide them to you ahead of time so that you know what to pay on the day of closing.

Lock Changes
While no one is forcing you to do this, you might want to! You don't know how many people may have keys to your new home, including the

previous owners. For your and your property's security and peace of mind, it's best to change the locks, or at least, rekey them.

MOVING COSTS

Think about budgeting for the cost of moving and what you will need when you move into your new home.

HELP FOR FIRST-TIME HOME BUYERS

Let's have a look at what kind of assistance a first-time buyer, such as yourself, can expect.

HOME BUYERS' PLAN

To buy a home, you need a mortgage, and to get a mortgage, you will need a minimum *down payment* of 5 percent. This may be different depending on where in Canada you live. The Home Buyers' Plan (HBP) was developed to help first-time home buyers save for a down payment. It allows you to withdraw up to $25,000 from your *Registered Retirement Savings Plan* (RRSP) to be used toward the purchase of a home. There is a payback period over fifteen years, whereby you must contribute the funds back into your RRSP. If you don't, then the repayment for that year gets reported as income when you file your income tax return.

How do you estimate your payments? Take your withdrawal amount and divide it by fifteen years.

Therefore, if you withdrew $25,000 divided by fifteen years, that equals $1,666.67 per year.

Note: Payback will start two years after the withdrawal. Funds from a Group RRSP will not qualify you for the Home Buyers' Plan; it must be from an individual RRSP. Be sure to read up on the rules and eligibility criteria before you withdraw the funds.

All in all, if you have the ability to take advantage of your RRSP, you should.

First-Time Home Buyers' Tax Credit (HBTC)

The HBTC is a federal government initiative designed to help eligible first-time home buyers cover some of the costs involved in purchasing a home, such as legal fees, disbursements, and land-transfer taxes. The maximum benefit is $750. You should speak to your Tax Preparer for more information on claiming this.

THE COSTS OF RUNNING A HOME

Besides the cost of buying a home, running a home comes with its own consistent expenses.

Here are some that you can consider:

Maintenance

There is no landlord. Whatever is needed to keep the home sound and in good order is now your responsibility.

Electricity and Gas

Now that you will have to pay for these utilities, perhaps you'll understand why your dad used to nag you to turn off unnecessary lights or appliances!

Water

Water does not magically come from the faucet; it is brought into your house from the municipal water supply before it flows through your open faucet. That costs money.

Furnace

The heating cost of your home is also an additional expense you should be aware of.

Telephone/Cable/Internet

This is obvious, no?

HOME INSURANCE

If you have a mortgage, then you have no choice. You must purchase home insurance. Common coverages are for the following:

- Liability (someone slips and hurts themselves on your property)
- Fire
- Water damage (be sure to inquire what type of loss is covered, as not everything may be)
- Sewer backup (check on this as well)
- Wind
- Theft
- And much more

Speak to an insurance professional to see what coverage is best for you.

As you can see, buying a home can be quite costly, not only for the home itself but also the daily upkeep of it. Be sure to crunch your numbers to ensure that you can not only afford the home but all the ongoing costs that come with it. If you have difficulties, speak to your family, your Realtor, or your financial advisor.

HELPFUL LINKS

For more information on help for first-time homebuyers, check out the following links:

Home Buyer's Plan

http://www.cra-arc.gc.ca/hbp/

First time home buyer tax credit (HBTC)

http://www.cra-arc.gc.ca/gncy/bdgt/2009/fqhbtc-eng.html

CHAPTER 11

MORTGAGES

NOBODY I KNOW has ever been able to buy a home outright, so once you've found the right home to purchase, you will need to apply for a mortgage. Common lenders are banks; they are on every corner. Additionally, you can go to independent mortgage agents, who represent multiple lenders. I would recommend speaking to both as you shop around for the best rate as well as terms of the mortgage.

QUALIFYING FOR A MORTGAGE

Mortgage lenders will look at a few criteria when they consider your mortgage application.

There are some steps you can take to ensure they approve it.

- Save or find enough for a down payment. This is where the *Home Buyers' Plan* can help you. If you use it and are only able to put down the minimum 5 percent deposit, your mortgage will be considered *high-ratio*, which means you are borrowing more than 80 percent of the home's value, and you will need to take out *mortgage insurance* (I will explain this in a bit). A conventional mortgage requires at least a 20 percent down payment.
- Make sure you earn enough every month to make your regular payments. Total up all your debts and expenses and calculate if you will be able to afford mortgage payments. Lenders require your monthly housing costs to be 32 percent or less of your *gross*

income. Housing costs include your mortgage payments as well as your taxes and heating costs. This is typically called your GDS ratio.

- Get rid of other debt. If you already owe a lot of money, you may not qualify for a mortgage. For Canadian lenders, your whole debt load should be less than 40 percent of your gross monthly household income. This is commonly called TDS ratio.
- Besides getting rid of debt, make sure your credit history doesn't let you down. Lenders will look into it to see how efficiently you pay your bills. If you have any bad credit, you may not qualify for a mortgage, or you may qualify for one at a very high interest rate! Another option would be if a relative, who meets the lender's criteria, would agree to be a guarantor or cosigner. While this is great, the interest rate may still be less than ideal.
  - Keeping your credit score high is relatively simple. Just be sure to pay off any balances on time. Even if you can't pay off the entire balance, pay the minimum amount on time. This will at least show your ability and willingness to pay debt on time—which is important to someone lending you hundreds of thousands of dollars!
  - If you find yourself in a situation where you can't pay the minimum balance, speak to the company and inform them—try to work it out with them. If they send collections after you, then it could really hurt your credit score.
- Make sure you have all necessary documentation conveniently compiled and available. This would include proof of where your down payment is coming from; details about your employment and salary, confirmed in writing by your employer or via pay stubs; details of your bank account(s), loans, and debts; proof of any financial assets such as policies or shares; and your driver's license.

Note: All lenders have their own criteria for GDS and TDS ratios, credit rating, and other lending criteria, which may affect your qualification for a mortgage. Some lenders may be more lenient then others.

MORTGAGE LOAN INSURANCE AND THE CMHC

Mortgage loan insurance protects the lender and in doing so makes it possible for borrowers who can't afford high down payments to be able to buy homes at affordable interest rates.

There are two main mortgage insurance companies: Canada Mortgage and Housing Corporation (CMHC) and Genworth Canada.

The CMHC serves as a public mortgage insurer, among other things. They are mainly active in markets and housing options not served by private insurers, including rural communities, multiunit residential properties, student and nurse housing, and retirement homes.

Lenders will only lend up to 80 percent; therefore, mortgage insurers will lend the additional amount between 80 percent and your down payment. If your down payment is 5 percent, then the mortgage insurers will lend the additional 15 percent (the mortgage lender lends 80 percent). You pay a premium on the extra 15 percent, which gets added to your mortgage payments.

MORTGAGE TERM

The *mortgage term* is the period (usually in years) in which the conditions of the mortgage have legal effect. After the term ends, you will have to renew at a new set of conditions prevalent at that time.

MORTGAGE INTEREST RATES

A *fixed mortgage interest rate* is one that will not be raised during the duration of the mortgage term. If you were to break this mortgage, the fees could be quite large. Be sure to ask what the breakage fees would be.

A *variable mortgage interest rate* may go up or down according to changes in the prime rate. If you were to break this mortgage, the fees would usually be only three months' interest. Be sure to ask what the breakage fees would be.

CLOSED MORTGAGE

A *closed mortgage* means you can't make more than the agreed monthly payments, and you may not pay off all or part of the mortgage before the end of the term, unless your mortgage has a condition whereby you can do so (e.g., by doubling up payments).

OPEN MORTGAGE

The flexibility of an *open mortgage* allows you the option of paying off part or all of the mortgage at any time. While this sounds great, it usually comes with a higher interest rate. Usually payments are interest only.

AMORTIZATION

Amortization refers to the period over which the whole mortgage debt will be paid off. This is typically twenty-five years. The advantage of a longer amortization period is that your scheduled payments will be lower. The downside is that you will pay considerably more in interest.

PAYMENT SCHEDULE

Mortgage loans are repaid in regular installments, such as monthly, biweekly, biweekly accelerated, weekly, or weekly accelerated. Although monthly is the most convenient for most homeowners, paying more frequently has benefits. The extra payment via the accelerated route helps reduce principal faster.

Hopefully now you have a better understanding of how a mortgage works. Be sure to sit with a mortgage specialist to fully understand the term and type of mortgage you are applying for. Before you sign your mortgage application you should know the term, rate, type (open/closed, fixed/variable rate), prepayment conditions, and how much it would cost to break the mortgage. Fully understanding your mortgage is important as you will likely have one for the next twenty-five years!

HELPFUL LINKS

For more information on mortgage insurer, Canadian Mortgage Housing Corporation (CMHC) check out https://www.cmhc-schl.gc.ca/

CHAPTER 12

UNDERSTANDING INVESTMENT ACCOUNTS AND OPTIONS

ONE OF THE most common things you will encounter as an adult is where and how to invest your money. There are many ways to invest, and in this chapter, I will introduce you to the main ones.

STOCKS

The stock exchange is basically a marketplace where *stocks* (also called shares), *bonds*, and other commodities can be bought and sold.

The holder of a stock has an ownership interest in a company. Stockholders can earn a return from their stock by selling its shares on the stock exchange for a price higher than what they bought them for. They can also hold onto shares of a stock and receive dividends. Dividends are a way that companies distribute profits among their shareholders. Not all companies can pay dividends regularly; it depends on the financial performance of the company at a given time.

You can manage your own portfolio, or you can pay a broker to trade on your behalf or an advisor to advise you on the trades to make.

MUTUAL FUNDS

Mutual funds are professionally managed investments, which pool together money from many investors, and invest this money into various stocks, bonds, and other asset classes. The fund manager picks the stocks that are held by the fund portfolio, adhering to a specific investment mandate. For example, a Canadian equity fund may mandate that up to 90 percent of the stocks invested in the fund must be Canadian stocks. By investing through mutual funds, you are holding a portfolio of many stocks and other assets, thus increasing your diversification. This allows you to benefit from the weighted return on the stocks invested within the fund versus only a few stocks if you were to buy them separately.

EXCHANGE-TRADED FUNDS (ETF)

ETFs typically track indexes, commodities, and other securities. The difference between a mutual fund and an ETF is that that you can own shares in an ETF, and these shares can be traded daily like stocks are, through a broker or dealer. Some ETFs provide diversification by tracking indexes, while others may not. An ETF tracking the Toronto Stock Exchange can give you diversification, but an ETF tracking the price of gold will not. The last thing to note about an ETF is that there is no active professional management—remember, they simply track other indexes and securities.

REGISTERED ACCOUNTS

Registered accounts are savings accounts that enjoy tax-preferred status. The main aim of registered accounts is to encourage people to save.

There are different types of registered accounts. I will introduce some of the main ones.

RRSP AND SPOUSAL RRSP

A *Registered Retirement Savings Plan* (RRSP) is a Canadian account for saving and holding various investment assets.

RRSPs must comply with certain stipulations of the *Income Tax Act*. There are restrictions to maximum contributions and the types of assets allowed within the account. By age seventy-one investors must convert to a Registered Retirement Income Fund (RRIF).

If you are contributing to your own RRSP, this is known as an *Individual RRSP*.

One of the main benefits of an RRSP is the tax advantage. By investing in an RRSP, your contributions are deductible against your income when you file your income tax return. This allows you to pay less in taxes. The earnings within an RRSP are also tax-deferred until redeemed. When you withdraw from your RRSP, the withdrawal gets added to your income in the year you withdraw, and you pay tax on that amount.

When you withdraw from an RRSP, you may be subject to withholding tax. Current withholding tax rates as of 2016 are as follows:

- 10 percent (5 percent for Quebec) on amounts up to and including $5,000
- 20 percent (10 percent for Quebec) on amounts over $5,000 up to and including $15,000
- 30 percent (15 percent for Quebec) on amounts over $15,000

Therefore, you should think twice before contributing to and withdrawing from your RRSP. Ideally, you should keep the money invested in the RRSP for your retirement.

A *Spousal RRSP* allows the higher-earning partner to contribute to an RRSP in his or her spouse's name. It is a means of dividing investments between the two spouses so that their retirement income is also split, thus making their joint marginal tax rate less than what it would be if only one of them earned all the income. When contributing to a Spousal RRSP, the contributor can still deduct the RRSP contribution from his or her own income tax return.

RRSPs also have two programs that you can take advantage of.

HOME BUYERS' PLAN

As discussed earlier, the Home Buyers' Plan allows a qualified first-time homebuyer to withdraw funds from his or her RRSP tax-free up to $25,000. However, this needs to be paid back over fifteen years.

LIFELONG LEARNING PLAN

This allows qualified individuals to withdraw funds from their RRSP tax-free to use toward full-time training or education for them or their spouses/common-law partners. You can redeem up to $15,000, and the contributions must be paid back over ten years.

Source: Canada Revenue Agency, http://www.cra-arc.gc.ca/

For both programs, if you do not make payments back into your RRSP, the "payment" for that given tax year will be added to your income and taxed as if you withdrew it from your RRSP.

TAX-FREE SAVINGS ACCOUNT (TFSA)

Canadian residents eighteen years and older can save or invest through the TFSA. Unlike RRSP contributions, those made to TFSA accounts are not deductible from taxable income. However, the income earned on contributions is not taxed, and neither is the money when withdrawn. Money may also be withdrawn from the account at any time.

As a TFSA account holder, you are the only one who can make contributions and withdrawals or decide how to invest the funds.

TFSA CONTRIBUTION ROOM

The *TFSA contribution room* limits the amount you can contribute to your TFSA. The maximum contribution for 2017 is set at $5,500. If you

Years	TFSA Annual Limit	Cumulative Total
2009-2012	$5,000	$20,000
2013-2014	$5,500	$31,000
2015	$10,000	$41,000
2016	$5,500	$46,500
2017	$5,500	$52,000

*This chart is accurate for Canadian residents who were at least eighteen years old as of 2009. Your TFSA contribution room starts in the year you turn eighteen.

don't contribute, your room accumulates. If you haven't contributed to a TFSA since 2009, you would have accumulated $52,000 contribution room. Fig. 4 shows the contribution totals.

DO NOT OVERCONTRIBUTE

Once you withdraw funds from your TFSA, you cannot contribute them back in the same year, unless you have additional contribution room. At the start of the following year, your room will reset, and you will be able to contribute what you withdrew back into your TFSA.

If you happen to overcontribute, you may have to pay a 1 percent penalty on the overage amount for each month you have over contributed!

Be sure to keep track of your room and check your account with the Canada Revenue Agency to find out about your limits.

LIRA/LRSP

A Locked-In Retirement Account (LIRA) and the very similar Locked-in Retirement Savings Plan (LRSP) are investment accounts for retirement, transferred from an employer's Registered Pension Plans.

The distinction between these accounts and a regular RRSP is that RRSPs can be cashed in at any time, while these accounts cannot. Also, once funds are transferred from a pension plan into a LIRA/LRSP, that's it—no further funds can be deposited. Their purpose is to hold your former pension funds and keep them locked in for you or your surviving spouse or partner. The funds only become available when the account holder retires or at an age specified in the relevant pension laws. Age fifty-five is the earliest where the funds can be either partially unlocked (moved to an RRSP and withdrawn) or converted to a LIF (Life Income Fund), where you can take the minimum or maximum payments from the account. Since this was formerly pension money, the legislation was created to hopefully allow the funds in this plan to pay out from the age of retirement throughout the remainder of a person's life.

There are other ways to unlock the funds earlier, but they are only meant for extreme circumstances—for example, coming into financial difficulty. A formal request must be made to the governing body to unlock the funds early.

HOW TO INVEST

DISCOUNT BROKERAGES
The arrival of the Internet made possible an electronic trading platform that gave rise to the affordable *discount brokerages*. A *discount brokerage* is a business offering clients online stock and security trading opportunities, for considerably lower fees, but also fewer services than traditional brokerage firms. Until they came along, only the wealthy could afford brokerage fees.

Discount brokerages provide sophisticated electronic trading platforms on which clients can run their own trading accounts with little or no interaction with a live broker. To experienced traders this is all they need, but for novice traders, it can be a daunting task.

INVESTING THROUGH YOUR BANK

You will have access to the same or very similar securities that you would online, through a discount brokerage. Many banks themselves have their own online discount brokerage platforms. However, you could also choose to work through the bank's securities advisor. Just be sure to find out how they are being compensated from your investment. Usually it is a percentage of the assets under management or a flat fee. Be sure to inquire about the services they will be providing you.

INVESTING WITH A FINANCIAL ADVISOR WHO PROVIDES INDEPENDENT FINANCIAL ADVICE

The key is to find a financial planner or advisor you feel comfortable working with, whether they work for a bank or a dealer. Most financial advisors are self-employed and are building their own client base. Therefore, the degree of knowledge they may have could be the same or greater than that of a bank's counterpart. They may have access to investments a bank may not, and they may also provide services outside of investments, such as insurance, tax preparation, mortgages, and real estate.

The bottom line is that your financial advisor should be happy to give you all the answers and offer all the advice you need to make smart choices. Be sure to communicate openly with your advisor and discuss goals and strategies. Periodically review your portfolio with your financial advisor to ensure you are receiving the best advice.

HELPFUL LINKS

For more information on the topics discussed in this chapter, see the following:

Life Long Learning Plan

http://www.cra-arc.gc.ca/tx/ndvdls/tpcs/rrsp-reer/llp-reep/menu-eng.html

Registered Retirement Savings Plan

http://www.cra-arc.gc.ca/tx/ndvdls/tpcs/rrsp-reer/rrsps-eng.html

Spousal RRSP

http://www.cra-arc.gc.ca/tx/ndvdls/tpcs/rrsp-reer/cntrbtng/spsl-eng.html

Tax-Free Savings Account

http://www.cra-arc.gc.ca/tfsa/

RRSP Withholding Tax on Withdrawals

http://www.cra-arc.gc.ca/tx/ndvdls/tpcs/rrsp-reer/wthdrwls/rts-eng.html

CONCLUSION

We began this journey together twelve chapters ago. Congrats! You made it this far. Not only have you learned everything you didn't learn in school but a few things many adults around you still don't know! To end this book, I'll keep it short and sweet. Every day wake up and be the best version of yourself. Continue learning and stepping outside of your comfort zone. Don't be afraid of what you don't know and embrace the challenges along the way. At times life will throw you curveballs but have the confidence in yourself to know that you will find a way.

The real world is complex, ever-changing, dynamic, but so exciting and fun! I am confident that you can totally do this whole, you know, adult thing, and hopefully any concerns or intimidating aspects of entering the adult world are now lessened. Everything You Didn't Learn in School aims to provide you with the knowledge you need to successfully navigate the big, bad, but exciting world of adults. Remember, this book is intended as an introduction, as each topic could be its own book entirely, so be sure to stay well informed! By reading this book, you're already ahead of the game, continue being proactive and keep asking questions.

Be smart and stay ahead of the crowd.

www.ingramcontent.com/pod-product-compliance
Lightning Source LLC
Chambersburg PA
CBHW060646210326
41520CB00010B/1762